INDONESIA

TIGER BOOKS INTERNATIONAL

Text by
Pietro Tarallo

Graphic design
Anna Galliani

Map
Cristina Franco

Contents

1 *The legong kraton, introduced in Bali around 1915, is an exceptionally difficult and elegant dance. Dressed in tight, ankle-length costumes made of fine, gaily coloured material embellished with gold thread, the dancers cannot move freely backwards and forwards. They nonetheless create the impression of constant movement by gliding over the ground with short, quick steps, keeping their knees bent and back arched, gracefully moving their head and arms and flicking their eyes from side to side.*

2-3 *Bali, "island of the gods", is the main centre of Hinduism in Indonesia. The Hindu religion and culture became an integral part of the native culture about 2,000 years ago, brought to the archipelago by Indian merchants and sailors whose routes took them across the Sunda Strait. Numerous religious festivals and ceremonies take place during the year: on these occasions long processions carry rich votive offerings to the temples.*

4-5 *Lombok is hemmed in by Sumbawa to the east and Bali to the west. At its widest point this almost square island is about 50 miles across. An imaginary line, traced by the English naturalist Alfred Russel Wallace in the second half of the* 19th century, *cuts the island in two: to the north-west the natural habitat is lush and equatorial; to the south-west it is impoverished and desert-like. Sengiggi Beach has for some years been the best known and most popular resort area on the island.*

6-7 *Farming is the main industry in the villages of Bali, and extensive use is still made of water buffalo and oxen. One of the wonders of the island is its complex irrigation system, which allows wet rice cultivation on terraced fields. Thanks to the favourable climate and very fertile volcanic soil, Balinese farmers almost always obtain two harvests a year.*

8 *The legong kraton dance narrates the complicated and dramatic story of the king of Lasmen and princess Lagnkasari.*

9 *Balinese native-style painting is known worldwide for its fascinating colours and the realism of its subjects, taken from traditional mythology and everyday life. Artists work with tempera on canvas, using a very distinctive style characterized by an all-pervading softness of tone. There are now art schools in many island villages; the most famous are situated in Ubud.*

This edition published in 1997 by TIGER BOOKS INTERNATIONAL PLC , 26a York Street Twickenham TW1 3LJ, England.

First published by Edizioni White Star. Title of the original edition: Indonesia, l'arcipelago infinito. © World copyright 1997 by Edizioni White Star, Via Candido Sassone 22/24, 13100 Vercelli, Italy.

ISBN 1-85501-872-1

Printed in Singapore
Color separations by Graphic Service, Italy.

South China Sea

MALAYSIA

SABAH

BRUNEI

SARAWAK

MEDAN

Samosir Island

Lake Toba

SUMATRA

KALIMANTAN
(BORNEO)

Mahakam River

BUKITTINGGI

PADANG

PONTIANAK

PALEMBANG

BANJARMASIN

Java Sea

INDONESIA

Sunda Strait

JAKARTA

TANJUNG PRIOK

BOGOR

SEMARANG

MADURA

BANDUNG

SURABAYA

LOMBOK

YOGYAKARTA

BALI

JAVA

DENPASAR

SUMBAWA

INDIAN
OCEAN

12-13 *Along the Bangsal coast on the island of Lombok are solitary, never-ending beaches, fringed with palms constantly ruffled by a gentle offshore breeze.*

14-15 *The mountainous inner regions of South Sulawesi, covering an area of about 231,660 square miles, are home to the Toraja (the name means people of the highlands, but literally just "highlands"). Today numbering about 760,000, they represent the proto-Malay segment of Indonesia's population.*

16-17 *Situated in the Sunda Strait between Sumatra and Java is Anak Krakatoa, "child" of the famous volcano which erupted with terrible force in 1883, causing the deaths of 36,000 people.*

18 top *Jayapura is the capital of Irian Jaya, the Indonesian part of New Guinea. It is also the gateway to the Baliem Valley, inhabited by the most interesting tribes to be found on this huge island.*

18 bottom *The tongkonam is the typical house of the Toraja of Sulawesi. Its shape resembles the boats used by the islanders. The high saddle-roof looks like the hull; it is made of layer upon layer of bamboo canes and is sometimes as much as seven feet thick.*

19 top *In the area around the town of Bukittinggi, in western Sumatra, live the Minangkabau. On ceremonial occasions the womenfolk wear eye-catching costumes made of brocade.*

19 bottom *Nutmeg and mace, cloves and cinnamon grow on the five tiny islands which together form the Banda archipelago. Western-style ramparts testify to their colonial past.*

21 *Not far from the Balinese village of Bedugul, a pathway leads to the shores of Lake Bratan, set in the crater of an extinct volcano. Often shrouded in mist, the lake is an important source of water for the entire region.*

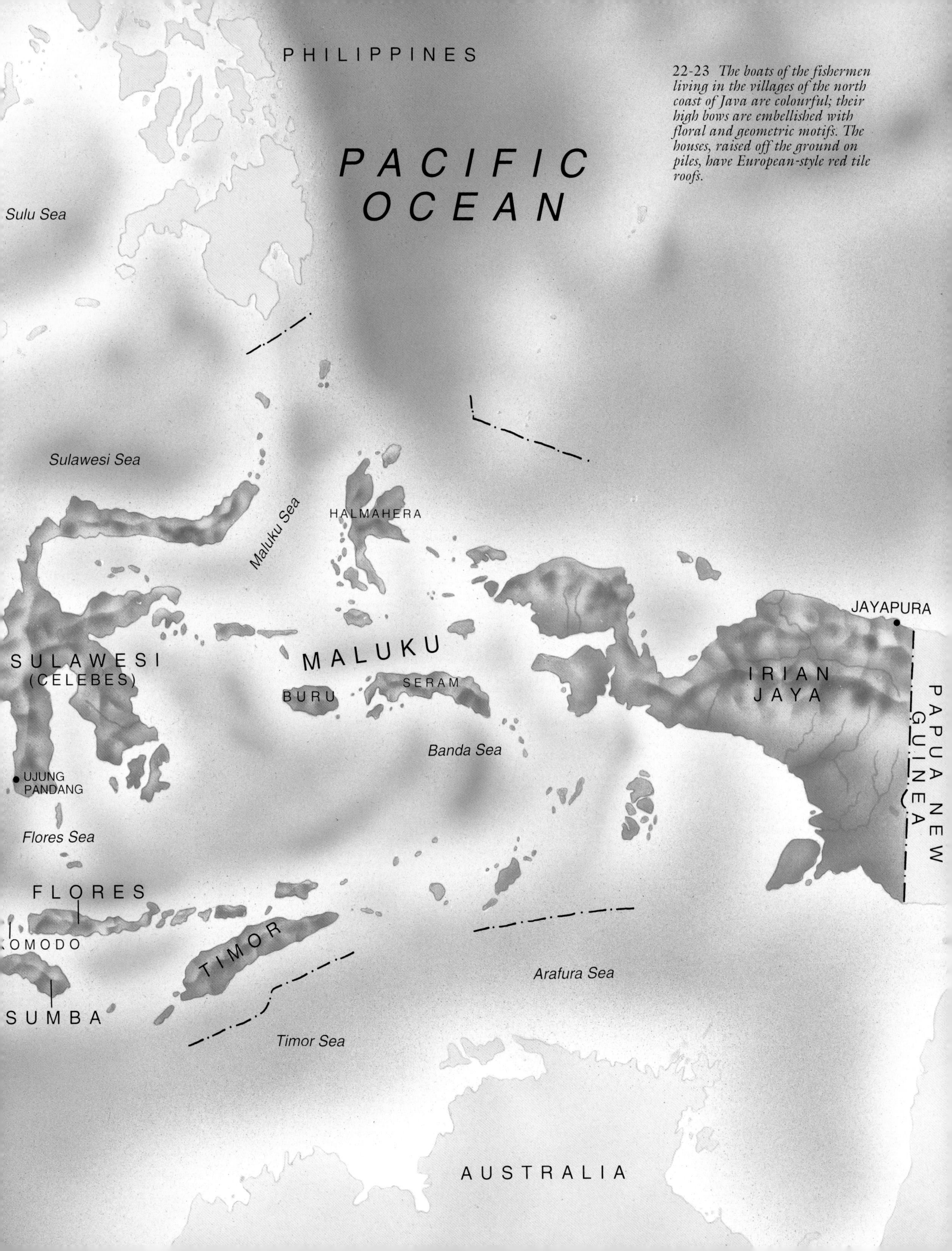

PHILIPPINES
PACIFIC OCEAN
Sulu Sea
Sulawesi Sea
Maluku Sea
HALMAHERA
MALUKU
SULAWESI (CELEBES)
BURU
SERAM
JAYAPURA
IRIAN JAYA
PAPUA NEW GUINEA
Banda Sea
UJUNG PANDANG
Flores Sea
FLORES
KOMODO
TIMOR
SUMBA
Arafura Sea
Timor Sea
AUSTRALIA

22-23 *The boats of the fishermen living in the villages of the north coast of Java are colourful; their high bows are embellished with floral and geometric motifs. The houses, raised off the ground on piles, have European-style red tile roofs.*

Introduction

Indonesia is the largest island complex in the world, an archipelago of over 17,800 islands, only 6,000 of them inhabited. There are some 30 minor archipelagoes and five huge islands: Java, Sumatra, Kalimantan (the Indonesian part of Borneo), Sulawesi and Irian Jaya (the west half of New Guinea). This immense arc of islands covers a total area of 752,405 square miles. It stretches east-west for 3,182 miles between the Malay peninsula and Australia, dividing the Pacific from the Indian Ocean: a bridge of land between Asia and the newest New Continent.

The geological structure of Indonesia is the final outcome of movements of the Earth's crust during the Cenozoic era. The lands which now form the Greater and Lesser Sunda chains emerged after a great geosyncline which produced the mountain ranges of Europe and Asia. As the folds which formed the Himalayas extended eastwards, they came up against pressure from the massifs of Southern China and Central Indochina: the product of this upheaval was the supporting structure of the Malay Peninsula and the semisubmerged Sunda Shelf. The configuration assumed by these folds in the end part of the arc of islands is extremely complex, since the last tectonic waves "broke" against the Archean Australian continental mass. Caught between these two opposing masses, the Indonesian islands acquired unique and complicated mountain systems, as well as strange shapes, like those of Sulawesi and the Maluku islands.

Volcanic activity is a fundamental characteristic of the Indonesian landscape, together with intensive seismic activity. There are about 300 volcanic cones, most of them active, concentrated particularly on the island of Java. Many of the volcanoes rise to heights of over 9,842 feet. This "belt of fire" - part of the much vaster volcanic ranges of the Pacific region - encompasses the entire country. Flowing lava, volcanic explosions and earthquakes are an ever-present reality for the people of Indonesia, something they learn to live with from early childhood.

Until August 28, 1883, the volcano Krakatoa stood at the centre of the island of the same name, 31 miles off the eastern coast of Java. On that fateful day, after weeks of unquiet activity, it erupted with greater explosive force than an atomic bomb. A tidal wave more than 98 feet high rose up and swept inland, destroying everything in its path for 15 miles. Over 36,000 people lost their lives. For more than 90 days the sun remained hidden behind a thick curtain of smoke. The storm of ash thrown out during the eruption circled the Earth seven times. Disembowelled by the tremendous explosion, the island sank, leaving only a few sharp rocks emerging from the surface of the water.

Decades later, in 1928, a kind of miracle happened: in this same place marked by death, Anak Krakatoa, offspring of the sunken volcano, first appeared from beneath the sea. The small cone slowly grew to its present height of 656 feet. Perhaps, in the space of 200 years, it will be as dangerous as its father.

On the island of Flores, some 1,243 miles away, Mount Kelimutu reveals a more enchanting side of nature. Set like precious gems in the volcano's craters are three lakes of different colours. The dark-green lake is separated by a ridge of jagged rocks from its neighbour, which is turquoise blue. Only a strip of lunar-like terrain divides them from the third lake, the largest and most foreboding, its waters as black as pitch. Geologists have never managed to find an explanation for the colour of the lakes. It is probably due to the volcanic minerals, lava and mix of gases present in the basins. Another unsolved mystery is that every ten years - the last time was in 1995 - the lakes change colour: the black one turns red while the green and blue ones "swap" colours.

The Indonesian islands rest on a marine shelf. The sea all around them has an average depth of only 180 feet and only rarely reaches 656 feet. Were the level of the sea to suddenly drop, even by as little as 33-66 feet, a large area of the shelf's continental mass would be exposed on the western side of the archipelago. Only the islands to the east - Sulawesi and the Lesser Sunda chain, separated from Borneo and Java by the deep Straits of Makassar and Lombok - would be unaffected. Along the many deep-sea trenches scattered in the eastern part of the archipelago are myriad groups of islands, elongated in shape and often assembled in arc-shaped patterns, fringed by rocks and coral reefs. Every kind of vessel can be seen in these usually calm waters: fishing boats, seagoing canoes with outriggers, cargo ships loaded with fine-quality timber, spices and copra, but also fast-moving boats with square, black sails, crewed by the latest generation of the pirates who have long infested these waters.

For all their splendour, the coral reefs are not without perils, in the form of long, yellow-striped sea snakes, for example, as well as sharks, manta rays and stinging coral ("fire" coral being the most dangerous). The walls of the reefs plunge vertically and dizzingly to a depth of 3,281 feet. As the water gets deeper, the scenario very quickly changes. All around are thousands and thousands of fish, of countless species and colours. Off the shores of Manado, in the north of Sulawesi, the islands of Bunaken, Siladen and Manado Tua have "sea gardens" of unrivalled spectacular appeal.

The wet regions of the west offer the ideal environment for the equatorial rain forests which cover 64% of the country's land surface. About 40,000 species of plants grow here, including 250 types of bamboo, 150 varieties of palm; hibiscus, jasmine, allamanda, bougainvillea, lotus and orchids; towering trees, among them valuable timber varieties like teak, ebony, sandalwood and banyan; the world's largest flowers, like *Rafflesia Arnoldi*, which can grow to a metre and a half in diameter, and *Amorphophallus Titanum*, which stands over 3 feet high; plus medicinal herbs of every kind, their magical properties known only to natives of the local villages.

Eastwards, forests become more scarce, and much

drier regions are encountered, with vegetation very similar to the sort that predominates in Australia: there are extensive stretches of savanna and xerophilous tree species. On some islands of Indonesia (Eastern Java, Lesser Sundas, regions of Borneo) savanna has replaced the primeval forest: since its destruction by fire at the hands of nomad farmers, rainfall has been insufficient for it to get re-established. *Alang-alang* (*Imperata cylindrica*) is one of the grasses that thrive here; some, like *Saccaharum spontaneum*, grow to heights of seven to ten feet.

In regions where the jungle has survived, forests extend to an elevation of 3,280-4,920 feet. Species growing above this height are typical of temperate climates: oaks, laurels and pine trees together with raspberries, strawberries, bilberries and violets. The scenery looks almost alpine. Below 3,280 feet, there are musaceae, zinzibers (ginger and cardamom), begonias, bromeliaceae and Christmas roses, as tall as young trees, forming a tangled maze of striking shapes and colours. Along the coasts there are luxuriant mangrove swamps, as well as the proverbial palms. As trees go, palms are - in effect - one of Indonesia's greatest assets. They come in numerous species, suited to different natural environments: in the lowlands we find *Corypha umbraculifera* and *Corypha gelanga*; in wetter places, particularly on Java and Sumatra, the nipa palm flourishes; common just about everywhere is the areca palm, which produces betel nuts; the sago palm (*Metroxylon sagus*) thrives in the more easterly islands. And all over Indonesia there are coconut palms and climbing palms, like the rattan which winds its creeping stems around nearby plants and is used in countless ways by indigenous populations.

Many creatures find in the wilds of the Indonesian rainforests their natural habitat: monkeys of every kind, insects, brightly coloured birds and butterflies, parrots, reptiles, buffaloes, tigers, rhinoceroses, elephants and crocodiles. Yet many species of the animal community have been the victims of indiscriminate slaughter and are now on the verge of extinction. Among the numerous initiatives taken to protect wildlife, the Indonesian government has established no fewer than 210 national parks and nature reserves.

Also for the "men of the woods" (as the orang-utan are called in Indonesian), the threat of extinction is very real. Only 6,000 or so of these shaggy, reddish-haired anthropomorphic primates - an endemic species of Sumatra and Borneo, whose genetic make-up is very similar to man's - still survive in the wild. To save them from complete extinction the Orang-Utan Rehabilitation Centre was founded in 1973 by Regina Frey and Monica Borner, two naturalists from the Zoological Society of Frankfurt, and set up on the banks of the river Bohorok, a few kilometres from Medan (Sumatra). The centre is now operated by the PHPA, the Indonesian government agency responsible for environmental conservation, and it is part of the vast Gunung Mount Leuser Taman National Park. During the dark years of Dutch colonization, young orangs were treated like exotic pets and paraded like dogs. Today unscrupulous traders still dispatch them to zoos all over the world. In their expressions and movements these gentle, placid creatures bear a disarming resemblance to humans. The adult male can attain a height of 59 inches and weigh up to 220 pounds, while the female is about half that size. They can move at great speed thanks to their long arms (with a span of 98 inches), leaping from tree to tree and climbing or walking on the branches. Their thumbs are short but they have big, strong fingers. Each night they build a new nest in the trees, bending branches to make a "bed" from a thick layer of leaves. Here they sleep in a position often assumed by man: supine with an open hand under their head. Females reach sexual maturity at the age of ten and remain fertile until 30. They have only one baby every six years and watch over it, with loving care, until it is ten years old.

Ujung Kulon National Park, on the Panaitan peninsula in south-west Java, is Indonesia's best known and most important wildlife reserve. Deep in its virgin forest (the name Ujung Kulon in fact means "virgin forest") live tigers, crocodiles, rare birds, a great variety of reptiles, iguanas and the last 60 surviving specimens of the Java rhinoceros. Indonesia is the only country in Asia where two species of rhinoceros can be found: the Java rhinoceros (*Rhinoceros sondaicus*) and the Sumatra rhinoceros (*Didermoceros sumatrensis*), of which there are still 780 specimens on the island. In the early nineties, specialists from the Asian Rhinoceros Group of the UICN Committee for Endangered Species, working in conjunction with the Indonesian government, decided to capture several specimens of the extremely rare Java rhinoceros to try to get these animals to reproduce in captivity. The objective was to re-introduce them in Way Kambas National Park in Sumatra. In addition, more effective surveillance measures were established to stop poachers killing rhinoceros for their horn, which can fetch a price of £ 32,000 per kilogram!

Another mythical creature is the so-called Komodo dragon. It got its picturesque name from the island where it was first discovered, but it also occurs on Padar and Rinca, two small islands between Sumbawa and Flores. This amazing reptile (known to science as *Varanus Komodoensis*) arouses primeval fears in both men and fellow beasts as it advances through the undergrowth, with gaping jaws and darting tongue. With 26 inward-slanting teeth on either side of its mouth, it can tear off pieces of meat weighing as much as 11 pounds, which it swallows without chewing. Its digestion works slowly and can take days; sometimes over a week goes by between one meal and the next. An astute and relentless hunter of deer, pigs, goats, rats and buffalos, this huge monitor lizard has a varied diet (it even eats turtle eggs) and does not disdain carrion. Besides four well-developed limbs, other morphological characteristics - like a rounded mouth and massive head - testify to its membership of the saurian family. Some of its features - the forked tongue used as a sensor when exploring the terrain, the shape of its vertebrae and its heart structure - have more in common with snakes. Eggs (25-30 in number) are laid in September by the females, in burrows five feet deep, and hatch in April. The newly-hatched young, about 20 inches long and weighing only 3 ounces, are defenceless little lizards which live in trees. Within 5-6 years they grow into

powerful dragons, 10-13 feet long and 300-330 pounds in weight, strong swimmers and astute hunters. They live for 50-100 years. The international scientific community first learnt of the existence of these mythical creatures in 1912 from Major A. Ouwens, Dutch director of the Botanical Gardens in Bogor (Java). The first scientific expedition to Komodo was organized by the New York Natural History Museum in 1926. But not until 1980 did these "dragons" really leave the world of myth, thanks to American researcher Walter Auffenberg and his many years of fieldwork. About 4,000 specimens now live in the park, these too at risk from the pressures of commercial exploitation.

The incredible variety of living species still to be found in this part of the globe involves the human race too. During the migratory waves of prehistoric eras, populations who inhabited the western regions of present-day Indonesia moved eastwards: today there are still traces of veddoid and negritoid peoples in tribes surviving in the heart of the Sumatra jungle. A subsequent wave brought Malays, who settled throughout the archipelago, pushing the Papuans into New Guinea. Scholars disagree about the theory of later migrations and the progressive settlement pattern of the present populations of the interior. What is certain is the common Asiatic origin of all the Indonesian peoples, generically classified as Malays. Many sedentary ethnic groups, settled in hilly and mountainous regions, are considered to belong to the proto-Malay race: these groups include the Bataks of Sumatra, the Niha of Nias, the inhabitants of the Mentawi islands, the Dayaks of Borneo and the Toraja of Sulawesi.

Once headhunters, these peoples are now peaceful farmers. In cleared forest areas, they grow tubers (yam, sweet potato, taro), fruit trees (bananas, durian, bread-fruit, pineapple) and numerous species of palm (coconut, sago, betel nut); millet and rice are cultivated in terraced fields, irrigated using ingenious systems supplied by rainwater. They rear pigs, chickens, oxen, buffalos and horses. They drink palm wine and rice and millet beer, smoke tobacco and chew betel. Their apparel is fanciful and shows a very definite taste for colour. Short skirts and loin-clothes made of bark, rotang fibre, palm leaves, ferns and grasses have now practically disappeared, replaced by garments made of cotton imported from India or woven locally on hand-looms. Ethnic groups (and social rank within groups) are differentiated by head-dress, religion or rank insignia, and clothes worn for ceremonies and festivities. A very popular garment - worn by men and women alike - is the *sarong*, a strip of brightly coloured cotton tied at the waist to form a loose, generally ankle-length skirt. A textile product typical of these islands, particularly Java and Bali, is *batik*, its elaborate designs created with a hot-wax coating process. *Ikat*, woven mainly in Flores and Sumba, is characterized by iridescent geometrical motifs or stylized representations of horses, dragons and lions. A varied range of weapons is used, from bows and blowtubes to firearms and metal weapons (particularly the *kris*, a dagger with a rigid serpentine blade). The once common practice of tatooing is now disappearing, save in a few areas like Kalimantan (where the

Dayaks use highly intricate and ornate designs) and the Mentawi islands (on Siberut patterns are essentially linear).

The social structure is based on exogamous clans, with marriage between two members of the same clan strictly forbidden. Most clans are patrilineal; only a very small minority are matrilineal.

Houses are rectangular or square, built of wood and bamboo and raised off the ground on piles; roofs, covered with leaves or grasses, are either sloping (Nias and Mentawi islands), or have upward-pointing ends (Batak) or saddleback (Toraja). Their exteriors are decorated with painted wood carvings: popular motifs are ships, buffalo horns or stylized mythological symbols. As well as individual family homes and rice barns, villages have communal longhouses, used by the village headman and visitors, as well as for religious ceremonies and funeral rites.

Through the ages the artistic spirit of these peoples has been expressed through stone. On occasions huge megaliths (dolmens, menhirs, sacrificial stones, stele, reliefs) were backbreakingly dragged from far-away places and pushed up on impervious slopes to the sites of villages (in Nias, Flores and Sumba).

Religious belief and practice among these populations point to total syncretism. Animism has been integrated with an elaborate series of beliefs populated by numerous deities, and veneration of dead ancestors. Ritual offerings and ceremonies are led by priests and priestesses whose skills as diviners and healers are still attributed to magic arts. In addition, Indo-Javanese Hinduism, Islam and Christianity have been strong influences.

The majority of the Indonesian population is of Neo-Malay origin and includes the peoples of Sumatra (Acehnese, Minangkabau and Lampung), Java and Madura (Sundanese, Javanese and Madurese), the Balinese, and the Bugis and Makassarese (of Sulawesi). These peoples have been profoundly influenced by the great civilizations of Asia (Indian, Chinese, Arab) and of Europe. In particular the culture of Islam (the Sunni branch has prevailed since the 17th century) has a very strong hold even today, and is entrenched in every aspect of social and cultural life. There are some important exceptions, however. Islam has not succeeded in changing ancient customs: the Minangkabau, for example, have maintained their matrilineal social structure; the Balinese still follow animistic beliefs, suffused with elements of Buddhism and Hinduism. A very sophisticated form of civilization developed among these peoples. Many traces of it are to be seen in the magnificent monumental architecture of Java: the great Buddhist temple of Borobudur, built in 850, and the 9th-10th century Hindu centre of Prambanan. It also materialized in arts and crafts, dance (most notably, in Java and Bali), theatre (with the *wayang kulit*, the shadow theatre and *wayang golek*, the puppet theatre), painting and weaving. The most famous epic poems of Indonesian literature also originated here.

Little trace is now left of the primitive Malays, but there still exist a few: the Punan tribes (Bukat, Basapan, Oloh-ot and others), believed to be the oldest inhabitants of Borneo, where they live in the central and northern forests, hunting wild game and trading hides, feathers, fruit

and rice; and the Afuri (or "men of the woods") of the Maluku islands, who are hunters and primitive farmers and among whom the influence of Australoid and Melanesian elements is plainly evident.

Indonesia is the fourth most populous country in the world. Official figures put its population at 192 million; according to certain estimates, however, there are as many as 195 million Indonesians, with a density of 98.5 inhabitants per square kilometre. The demographic increase stems from various related causes: women have an average of 3.5 children and the birth rate stands at 28 per thousand, with a natural increase of 18 per thousand.

The inhabitants of Indonesia are essentially young: 62% are aged under 30, only 9% over 65. In recent years the population has grown amazingly fast: in 1920 it stood at less than 50 million; by the beginning of World War II it had reached 70 million; in 1961, when the first census was taken, it was 96 million; in 1971 the figure was 119 million, in 1981 140 million. Continuing at the present pace, by 2001 Indonesia will have 216 million inhabitants.

About half the people of Indonesia are Javanese, which is why this ethnic group has dominated the nation's life, particularly since independence. The whole archipelago is in fact undergoing a process of "Javanization", encouraged by the government since the economy and major centres of power are in Javanese hands. There is also a fairly large Chinese community (about 6 million), essentially city-based traders.

The population is concentrated on Java (one of the world's most populous regions, with over 110 million inhabitants and a density of 884 inhabitants per square kilometre) and in the big cities (more than 9 million people live in Jakarta).

The world's greatest religions co-exist in Indonesia, together with ancestral beliefs and pagan deities. Islam, introduced by the Arabs, is the most widely professed religion (87%, making Indonesia the largest and most populous Muslim country in the world). Christianity has also made its mark here (9% of the population are Christian), particularly the Lutheran church, supported by the Dutch during their colonial period. The Protestant church has its biggest congregations - grouped together under the so-called Hkbp (Huria Krise'n Batak Protestan) - in Sulawesi and Sumatra; the people of Flores, Timor and Siberut are predominantly Roman Catholic. Animistic religions, which added layers of new "mainstream" religions to their traditional beliefs, continue to have followers. There are still communities of Hindus (1%, particularly in Bali) and Buddhists (3%, mostly Chinese). These two religions were introduced from India, and became established in Sumatra and Java as early as the 7th century. From the 13th century onwards they gradually succumbed to the slow but relentless penetration of Islam. In the early 16th century the Portuguese arrived here in search of spices and built fortresses in the Maluku islands (Ternate, 1534), Timor, Solor and Flores. With them came Franciscans, Dominicans and Jesuits who undertook the task of evangelizing these regions. About a century later the Portuguese were displaced by the Dutch who banned Roman Catholicism (until 1807 when Rome sent more

24 *Sulawesi - once called Celebes - is one of the loveliest and wildest islands of the Indonesian archipelago. On account of its strange shape, it has been likened to an orchid. More than half the island is covered by thick tropical vegetation, with lush forests stretching right down to the shores of the ocean. High-canopied, broad-leaved tree species are the most common (and include valuable timber varieties like teak, ebony and sandalwood), but there are also rubber trees and bamboo. The rain forest attracts an amazing assortment of fauna: small mammals, birds, butterflies of every imaginable colour and snakes, many of them extremely poisonous. Among the creatures endemic to Sulawesi are the babirusa - a cross between pig and deer - and the anoa, a dwarf buffalo about 39 inches high. In the north live five different types of macaques, a fact that makes this island unlike any other on earth.*

missionaries). The Dutch encouraged widespread introduction of the Protestant religion, until 1947 when Indonesia gained its independence and they left the country.

About 300 different languages and thousands of dialects are spoken across the Indonesian archipelago: an idiomatic Babel. The most dominant are Javanese and Sundanese, both of which originated in Java and spread throughout the islands as the kingdoms of Java became increasingly powerful. Their widespread use also testifies to the cultural supremacy of Java over the other Indonesian islands. The official language is Bahasa Indonesia, adopted to give the country a national language, a language of unity. This new language was officially embraced in 1928, during a congress of scholars and linguists, partly in response to pressure from political movements struggling for independence. This lingua franca was created ex novo, adding to a Malay base many loan words from Dutch, English, Arabic, Portuguese, Sanskrit and Chinese. It is still not the everyday language of Indonesian people at large, but it is taught in schools and used in business, trade and the public administration.

The Indonesian economy is shaped by a paradox common to many Third World countries: an immensely rich country, it remains underdeveloped. Indonesia has vast natural resources and foreign investments on a massive scale provide it with huge liquidity reserves. And yet, Indonesia has acquired only the infrastructure needed to facilitate the movement of raw materials from the inland regions of its islands to the coast; few investments have been made in basic industry and the manufacturing industry. Systematic exploitation of the country's resources started under Dutch rule, with plantations which grew the products needed in the Western world (tea, rubber, tobacco, sugar cane, coffee, spices) and extraction operations for tin, oil, bauxite, coal, etc. The economy is now expanding fast, as recent figures confirm: GDP per person has escalated, increasing more than tenfold in the last 25 years; the country is nearly self-sufficient in food production (today 15% of the population lives below the poverty line); inflation is fairly low. In 1995 the World Bank defined the country's growth as amazing and included Indonesia among the so-called HPAEs (High Performing Asian Economies), on a par with the most dynamic countries that are part of the "East Asian miracle". In 1996 Moody's, the international ratings agency, classified Indonesia in the BAA3 band, together with Greece, South Africa and India.

25 top *The equatorial jungle of Sumatra offers an ideal habitat for many forms of wildlife. But the island's animals, like its forests, have suffered indiscriminate slaughter and numerous species are now on the verge of extinction. A significant example is the indigenous tiger* (Panthera Tigris Sumatrae) *of which few specimens still survive. Much is now being done by international foundations and others, to protect the fauna of Sumatra and 210 reserves have been established on the island.*

25 bottom *The* Rafflesia Arnoldi *is the largest flower in the world, some specimens measuring five feet across. In the early stages of its growth it looks like a purple cabbage; it flowers for only a couple of days, in November-December - and when it dies, it gives off a nauseating smell of rotting flesh.*

26-27 *The reliefs on the upper and lower panels of the walls of the Borobudur - the huge Buddhist temple close to Yogyakarta, in Java - relate respectively events in the life of Prince Siddharta, the future Buddha, and legends regarding his former lives.*

28-29 *Jakarta, on the island of Java, is Indonesia's splendid but chaotic capital. This mega-city of the tropics teems with people: with its sprawling conurbation its population of 9 million grows to 11 million. The centre of Jakarta is crossed by a busy thoroughfare - Jalan Thamrin - flanked by high-rise luxury hotels and the gleaming offices of multinational businesses.*

The wonders of nature

30 top *Sumba - a mountainous island 25-43 miles wide and 130 miles long - is encircled by other islands with musical and magical names; its highest mountain, Wangga Meti, is 4,019 feet high. With its complex social structure, varied dwellings and intriguing traditions, Sumba is one of Indonesia's most interesting islands from a cultural and anthropological standpoint.*

30 bottom *Not far from Bukittinggi, in Sumatra, is Lake Maninjau. Its clear waters, in the crater of a once-active volcano, attract bathers and also abound in fish. One of the many species found in the lake is* bakar bambu cobek ikan, *which the restaurants along the shores serve grilled with peanut sauce. Visible in the distance is the blue profile of the volcano Mt. Singgalang (9,449 feet).*

31 *Rice fields are an ever-present feature of the Balinese landscape but the islanders also grow maize, tobacco, coffee and coconuts and they raise pigs, chickens, ducks, birds and cows. Peasants are members of farming co-operatives (subaks) and attendance at meetings held periodically to discuss problems is compulsory. A committee is elected to organize work, supervises the efficient functioning of irrigation systems and shares out produce, also organizing harvest festivities and preparing the ritual offerings for Dewi Sri, the goddess of rice.*

32-33 *The Dieng Plateau, on Java, extends to the south-west of Semarang and to the north of Wonosobo, about 81 miles from Yogyakarta. Situated at an elevation of 6,562 feet, it is surrounded by mountains and a cool climate, typical of mountainous regions, prevails here. The scenery is delightful: there are pine forests, stands of tropical trees, rice fields often precariously perched on steep hillsides, tobacco plantations, lakes with bubbling sulphur springs, craters of extinct volcanoes, boric acid fumaroles and thermal springs. On the plateau there were once many candis (or temples) but only eight have survived. All dedicated to the god Shiva, they date back to the 7th century and are probably the oldest on Java.*

33 top *Although the archipelago of Pulau Seribu is also known as "Thousand Islands", it actually consists of only 340 small islands, covered with coconut palms and fringed by coral reefs. It is situated some 37 miles from the coast, north of Jakarta, in the Java Sea. Still an exclusive resort, off the beaten tourist track, it is a favourite destination of wealthy weekenders from Jakarta.*

33 bottom *The Seribu islands can be reached easily in two or three hours by boat from Marina Ancol or from the ports of Tanjung Priok or Sunda Kelapa in Jakarta; there is also an airstrip on Pulau Panjang. The largest island is Pulau Bidadari, while the tiny Pulau Ayer is the most exclusive. Further north are the Seribu Paradise islands, these too of coral origin: countless colourful fish and iridescent shells make their sea beds a truly spectacular sight. On the most beautiful islands of the group - Pulau Putri, Pelangi, Perak and Papa Theo - the coral reefs and natural environment are still unspoilt.*

34-35 *The 25 active volcanoes on Java (out of a total of 121) probably date back to the Quaternary period. During the course of millenia they have left a determining mark on the island's geology and history. Lava and effusive materials may have made the soil fertile but catastrophic eruptions have brought death and destruction.*

35 top *Mt. Merapi, on Java, rising to a height of 9,550 feet, is one of the most terrible volcanoes on Earth: its periodical eruptions (every six years or so) have caused countless deaths and enormous damage. In 1006 the entire area around Borobudur (Java's Pompei) was laid waste for several generations. Local people believe the* volcano to be the home of deities and therefore consider it sacred. Every year, to appease it, the Sultan of Yogyakarta climbs up to the crater and throws down his garments and hair: this ritual echoes the mystical ascensions to the mountain-god made a thousand years ago by the Buddhist kings of the Saliendra dynasty.*

35 centre *Anak Krakatoa, "child" of the volcano Krakatoa which disappeared in 1883, was born in 1928: the small cone which slowly emerged from the sea now stands 656 feet high. In 200 years or so it may be as big and destructive as its father. Scattered around Anak in this stretch of sea, 31 miles off the* west coast of Java, *is a motley assortment of islets and rocks: they are the remains of the old volcano, now recolonized by flora and fauna. The face of Anak too continues to change: a tremendous eruption in 1980 signalled the resumption of its turbulent activity and a new crater - the fifth - appeared.*

35 bottom *One of the best known of Java's many active volcanoes is Bromo, which last erupted in 1930. Only smoke and steam now emerge from its crater but incandescent magma continues to froth deep in its bowels. Bromo is in fact a volcano-in-a-volcano. Over the course of time Nature has created an intriguing landscape: the chimney of Bromo emerges from a sea of sand, about 7 miles across, at the side of two extinct volcanoes (Batok with its deeply corrugated cone, and Widodaren) on the bottom of a much older and larger outer crater with walls over 328 feet high. The result is a spectacular geological phenomenon: viewed from above, the three craters of Bromo, Batok and Widodaren lie in the middle of a gigantic "bowl" with a sandy floor and raised sides.*

Sumatra, land of gold

36 top *Situated at 2,972 feet above sea-level, Lake Toba, of ancient volcanic origin, is the largest inland body of water in South-East Asia and one of the deepest in the world (1476 feet). Surrounding it are mountains and gently rolling hills clothed in pines and tropical trees: a magical setting for long walks through the woods.*

36 bottom *In Bukittinggi - an old colonial city and administrative centre of the Minangkabau people - Panorama Park affords great views over the spectacular Ngarai Sianok Canyon. At the bottom of this chasm, 328-394 feet deep, flows the meandering river Jaring while rice fields extend over large areas nearby.*
36-37 *Paddy fields surround the large*

communal houses of the Minangkabau. Raised off the ground on sturdy piles, these elongated buildings have curved, palm-thatched roofs with gables soaring upwards at either end, like the horns of a buffalo. The houses are built modular-style, adding extensions as and when the occupants increase in number and the women of the family marry (houses are inhabited by several

families of the same matrilineal line). The wooden exterior is decorated and carved: ornamental motifs are usually geometric or inspired by leaves and trees. There are painted shutters at the windows. The compound of houses includes rice barns and stables, these too with traditional curved roofs and pointed gables.

38 top *Situated a few miles from Medan, on the banks of the River Bohorok, is the Orang-Utan Rehabilitation Centre, set up to help apes which have spent their entire existence in contact with man, in circuses or on plantations, to readjust to life in the forest. Re-educating these creatures - which are often also in need of extensive medical treatment - is a long and difficult process.*

38 bottom *Kalimantan is the name used by Indonesians for their "two-thirds of Borneo", the third largest island in the world. The other third of Borneo is divided into the states of Sabah and Sarawak, belonging to Brunei and Malaysia respectively. The highest peak is Mt. Kinabalu, 13,455 feet, from which flow long, winding rivers of muddy water, the only means of access to the thick rain forests of the interior.*

39 top *The rain forest is Kalimantan's greatest resource, together with oil. Its trees have already been extensively "harvested" and many continue to be felled each year, for export as fine-quality timber. Mangroves and nipa palms are found along the coasts, bordering vast stretches of uninhabited swampland.*

39 bottom *The Ujung Kulon National Park - Indonesia's most famous nature reserve - occupies 62,500 hectares of land on the Panaitan peninsula, jutting into the waters of the Sunda Strait, directly opposite Sumatra. In the depths of its forests live tigers, crocodiles, rare birds, a great variety of reptiles, iguanas, the last 60 surviving specimens of the Java rhinoceros and possibly even the legendary white unicorn, long gone from every other part of the globe.*

40-41 *Ganesh is a pot-bellied, elephant-headed Hindu deity. It is thanks to this jovial, good-natured god, protector of merchants and lovers, that the elephant is a sacred and respected animal, even though often used for tiring work. A scheme introduced towards the end of 1982 forced two hundred wild elephants to leave the Southern Sumatra jungle in search of a new habitat. The trials and tribulations of these poor creatures started when the authorities began to grant permits to fell entire tracts of forest where there were trees of value for their timber. Day after day, the elephants suffered the consequences of the destruction of the only natural environment they knew: tracks they had trodden through the thick undergrowth, ponds and rivers where they drank, clearings where they found food.*

Bali, island of the gods

42-43 *Just 6 miles from Denpasar, Sanur is the island's best known tourist resort; it also enjoys a reputation that has spread beyond South-East Asia to the Western world. In the early years of this century it was still a tiny village, set off by the lush green of its many coconut palms. In the Thirties a number of foreign artists, captivated by its beauty, made their homes here. One of the first was the Belgian artist Le Mayeur de Merpres, who lived here for 26 years (from 1932 until his death in 1958). His house is still here, occupied by his widow, Ni Polok, a famous legong dancer. After her husband's death, she donated all his works to the Indonesian government, who founded a museum to house them. The Balinese people admire Sanur as a beauty spot but prefer not to live there, believing the place to be sacred to ocean spirits.*

43 top *Bali once enjoyed the mythical status of an island paradise with peaceful, deserted landscapes, breath-taking scenery, mysterious and colourful dances and rituals. In recent years many of the myths have faded away as Western lifestyles have started to take root among the local population. These profound changes are most evident in popular tourist centres like Denpasar, Kuta, Legian, Sanur, Nusa Dua. Here little is left of the former natural environment and social structure. The tourism industry is big business in Bali, attracting thousands of millions of dollars; it has also brought to the island foreign developers and entrepreneurs who have built holiday villages, luxury hotels, restaurants and nightclubs.*

43 bottom *In the far south of Bali the new frontier of international tourism continues to advance, for instance along the fabulous white beach of Nusa Dua, dotted with hotels that now have a total capacity of over 7,000 beds. The water is amazingly transparent here: close to the beach white coral reefs and a sea floor teeming with marine life make the site ideal for underwater exploration. Low tide reveals coral and shells of every imaginable shape and colour. Nusa Dua means "two islands", in reality two small headlands joined to the mainland by a strip of sand.*

44-45 *A unique succession of white coral beaches and black volcanic sands are set against a backdrop of palm trees, their fronds rustling in the wind. The sea, with its crystal-clear waters whose colour fluctuates from dark green to turquoise blue, and continuously rippled by the waves, has brightly colourful depths. While the thousands of temples testifying to Bali's Hindu culture draw many visitors, nature is the real key to the island's tourist appeal: with its pleasant climate, dazzling landscapes and picture-postcard beaches it has gained the reputation of being a "paradise island", "island of the gods", "island of dreams". This seemingly perfect place is now under threat from demographic escalation and the ever more numerous tourist developments. Repercussions at environmental level often destroy the profound and harmonious relationship that exists between man and nature. Also at risk are animal species: in recent years doubts have been voiced about the survival of the white Rothschild starling and the island's turtles.*

46 Rice growing is one of the
mainstays of the Balinese economy:
erupting volcanoes have made the
island's soil exceptionally fertile,
abundant rainfall and streams
provide the enormous water
resources needed and the many
months of sunshine during the dry
season ripen the crops for harvest.
Most of the irrigated areas are in
the central and southern parts of
Bali; the paddy fields pictured here
are near Gunung Kawi, ten miles
north of Ubud.

47 The countryside around
Tirtagangga, on the eastern side of
Bali, offers stunning scenery:
landscapes shaped by forests, gentle
slopes and foaming waterfalls
alternate with rice fields and
coconut palms. Prominent in the
background, in this photo, is the
mighty Mount Agung, the highest
mountain on the island, rising to
10,308 feet; this giant last erupted
in 1963 with devastating effects.

48-49 *Paddy fields are a ubiquitous feature of Balinese landscapes. They are often a spectacular sight, perched on terraced hillsides with the countless temples of the "island of the gods" reflected in their waters. Rice is the main staple throughout South-East Asia and particularly in Indonesia. It is eaten every day and is the basic ingredient of many delicious dishes. For instance,* nasi goreng, *fried rice served with onion, garlic, paprika, pulses, shrimps, small pieces of beef or chicken (as well as fried eggs, to order);* nasi campur, *boiled rice mixed with fried egg, beancurd, soybean shoots and pieces of chicken;* nasi putih, *boiled rice usually served with all other dishes.*

Jewels of the Pacific

50-51 *East of Sumbawa and west of Flores is the Komodo archipelago, formed of three main islands - Komodo, Padar and Rinca - plus a series of islets and a handful of rocks. The surrounding sea looks like a lake, framed by an infinite number of islands whose coasts appear to glide over the water like flowing lava. Etched on the horizon are the profiles of barren mountains. Here nature is revealed in its full splendour. Komodo is the most accessible of the islands and the most popular with tourists*

interested in wildlife, who come to see Varanus komodoensis, *the giant lizard. Together these almost entirely uninhabited islands form a national park where there are currently about 4,000 of the famous and still endangered lizards. The Komodo dragon is a terrifying sight: it moves slowly and cautiously through the undergrowth, with gaping jaws and darting tongue, ready to pounce on its prey with surprising speed. It is a basically lazy creature: by 8 a.m. it is up and on the move but around 11 o'clock it starts a long siesta, while waiting for the temperature to drop; not until 4 p.m. does it at last set off in search of food. The mating season is brief - late June to late July - but also fairly violent: the males attack their rivals in ritualistic but cruel combat, exchanging bites with greater ferocity than when fighting over food or supremacy in power struggles.*

52-53 *Mt. Kelimutu, deep in the interior of Flores, offers a breath-taking sight: three lakes set like precious gems in the craters of the volcano. Here only the cries of eagles break the silence. The lowest lake, dark green in colour, is separated from the turquoise blue one, slightly higher up, by a ridge of jagged rocks. Only a strip of barren land divides them from the third lake, the largest and most foreboding. Its still waters, black as coal, look impenetrable and hostile: a gaping hole into nothingness. According to local legend, the lakes are resting places for the souls of the dead: young people are destined for the turquoise-blue waters, the wise for the deeper green waters, sinners for black waters, where they suffer unutterable torment but on moonless nights they hover menacingly in the sky above, looking for anyone who dares to violate these places.*

54 top *Tidore, in the northern Maluku Islands, is slightly less known than nearby Ternate. Dominating its landscape is a volcano, Mt. Kiemtabu, its rocky profile omnipresent on the island's skyline. The colourful market held on Sundays in the small village of Rum draws crowds from neighbouring islands too.*

54 centre *The imposing houses of Sumba - like those on Nias Island (Sumatra) - have high-peaked roofs which soar skywards, shaped like pagodas or truncated pyramids. The dwellings are arranged in a circle around a large open area, as if to protect the ancient core of this people's religious beliefs and rites from prying eyes.*

54 bottom *An ancient Spanish colony, Flores is an elongated island lying in the sea not far from Komodo. Although it has many towns - Ende and Maumere being the most important - long stretches of totally uninhabited coast rise steeply out of the sea, broken by golden lagoons and deep inlets.*

54-55 *Beyond Maumere, the most important town on Flores, is the splendid beach of Pantai Waiara, its palm-fringed white sands stretching as far as the eye can see. In the transparent blue waters off the coast is a marine park where coral gardens teem with multicoloured tropical fish.*

56-57 *The fertile Baleim Valley is located in the central uplands of Irian Jaya, just an hour's flight from Jayapura. Thanks to the altitude (4,921 feet), the climate here is cool and temperate. The inhabitants of this region belong to Irian Jaya's most famous tribe: the Dani. The men continue to wear the traditional penis sheaths, the women their characteristic straw skirts.*

57 top *Wamena is the only town of some importance in the Baliem Valley. The Dani come to its market to trade their products for essential items.*

57 bottom *Puncak Jaya, or Mt. Carstensz (16,568 feet), is the highest mountain in the chain which divides the island in two lengthwise. Not far from here is Gunung Biji, with the rich Freeport copper mines and the nearby town of Tembagapura.*

58-59 *Here and there along the rivers of Irian Jaya, water escaping over low banks creates marshlands: a maze of swamps and canals thick with palustrine grasses. Places like these are the ideal habitat for reptiles: crocodiles, sometimes over 23 feet long, pythons and a highly poisonous viper whose bite causes instant death.*

Turning back through the pages of history

60 top *At the very heart of Jakarta stands the huge National Monument (Monas), a white Carrara marble obelisk over 328 feet high, topped by a gilt flame, erected to commemorate Indonesia's independence. From the very top (accessible to the public) there are fine views of the enormous Merdeka Square with gardens and fountains which reflect the glimmering lights of the surrounding skyscrapers and shopping centres.*

60 bottom *Padang is an important port and trading centre; with its approximately 590,000 inhabitants, it is the third largest city on Sumatra. As well as being the island's western capital, it is a focal point of the Muslim religion and culture, as yet little affected by tourism. Padang first developed in the 18th century when it became a prosperous centre of the thriving trade in gold and pepper. The town hall (shown here) has been built in the style of traditional Minangkabau houses, interpreted along rather more modern lines.*

61 *Ubud is the foremost centre of painting on Bali, renowned on international art markets. Some of the best Balinese artists were born in the town and continue to live here; from the Thirties onwards numerous foreign painters also settled here. About 2 miles from Ubud is the Monkey Forest, site of the Temple of the Dead; at the entrance to the temple is a statue of the evil witch Rangda, in the process of tearing young boys into pieces.*

Java, heart of Indonesia

62 top *Exhibited at the National Museum in Jakarta are objects representing the cultures which flourished in Indonesia between the 7th and 15th centuries; rare Chinese ceramics; jewellery, krisses, weapons, gold and silver wares; archaeological finds; ethnographic pre-historic remains including the skull cap of* Pithecanthropus erectus, *some 350,000 years old, discovered by Eugene Dubois in 1891 at Trinil, near Sangiran.*

62 centre *On the south side of Taman Fatahillah Square, in the heart of old Jakarta, is the Sejarah Jakarta Museum, which offers visitors a chance to delve deep into the history of Java during its colonial period under Dutch rule.*

62 bottom *Sunda Kelapa, Jakarta's old harbour town, extends beyond Pasar Ikan, its wharfs crowded with the many old schooners that still plough the Indonesian seas.*

62-63 *Jakarta - like Singapore, Bangkok, Hong Kong and Tokyo - is crowded with futuristic skyscrapers. Running south from the centre is the Jalan Thamrin, a long, wide thoroughfare which forms the city's business district and the focal point of international tourism. The best hotels are located here, as well as banks and representative offices.*

64 top *Yogyakarta lies 373 miles from Jakarta and 373 miles from Denpasar (Bali). It is situated only 15 miles from the Indian Ocean, in the middle of a plain which extends to the foot of the volcano Mt. Merapi. A meeting point of ancient civilizations since prehistoric times, it was from here that the Indian culture brought to Java in the first centuries A.D. spread to the rest of the island. Its powerful princes long dominated much of Java: both the celebrated Buddhist sanctuary of Borobudur (9th century) and the great Hindu monument at Prambanan (9-10th century) were built at their instigation. Islam also became firmly entrenched in Yogyakarta, its beliefs becoming part and parcel of the creative and religious spirit of the local people.*

64 bottom *In the 16th century Yogyakarta experienced a new period of splendour as the centre of the Islamic Kingdom of Mataram. All the sultans and princes of Java bowed to its authority and its kings succeeded in holding their own against Dutch expansionist forces until the mid-18th century. With conquest by the Dutch came the decline of Yogyakarta's political leadership of Java, although it* remained the country's artistic and cultural centre.
In recent decades the city was governed by the sultan Hamengkubuwono IX who established the personal bodyguard which often parades in front of the Kraton, the palace occupied by his dynasty. Upon his death in 1988 he was succeeded by his 16 year-old son Bangkubumi, who assumed the title of Hamenkubuwono X.

65 *Yogyakarta continues to have strong ties with ancient traditions. The very finest offerings in the way of dance, theatre, music and crafts, as well as* batik *and silverware production, are to be found here, making the city a popular destination for specialists and tourists alike. Particular attractions include performances of traditional dances, held in the Kraton, and the* wayang kulit *shadow puppet theatre.*

67 left *A prominent feature of the centre of Bukittiggi is the Jam Gadang clock tower, which dominates the large square with its covered market. Now a symbol of the town, the tower was built by the Dutch in 1827 to control the movements of the Minangkabau during the Padri war.*

67 top right *Standing on the central Jalan Diponegoro in Padang is the Adityawarman Museum, housed in a faithful copy of a Mingangkabau longhouse, flanked by rice barns* (rangkiangs). *It was opened in 1977. Exhibited here are collections of old and traditional objects, as well as examples of some of the finest and rarest fabrics made in this part of Sumatra.*

67 bottom right *In Bukittinggi even new buildings have traditional curved roofs, pointing upwards at either end like the horns of the buffalo.*
The town is situated in western Sumatra, at an elevation of 3,051 feet. It stands on a hill encircled by mountains and uncomfortably close to three volcanoes (Mounts Merapi, Sago and Singgalang) which represent a constant threat for the entire surrounding area.
The climate here is mild and the vegetation lush and inviting; nearby are large lakes (Maninjuau and Singkarak), while cultivated fields and trade are a source of wealth and prosperity for the local people.

66 *Siak Sri Indrapura is one of the many villages scattered along the southernmost coasts of Sumatra. Its wooden houses, raised off the ground on tall stilts, have been inhabited for generations by fishermen and boatmen familiar with all the secrets of these seas, which are often made treacherous by currents and sudden storms.*

Borobudur,
treasure of the Buddha

68-69 *The great Buddhist temple of Borobudur was built around 850 A.D. under the Saliendra dynasty and abandoned some 150 years later. Vegetation eventually caused the deterioration of the complex: bit by bit woody lianas, lichen, moss and roots dislodged the stones which eventually began to crack and disintegrate.*

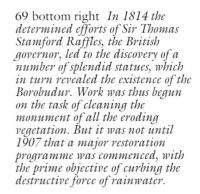

69 bottom right *In 1814 the determined efforts of Sir Thomas Stamford Raffles, the British governor, led to the discovery of a number of splendid statues, which in turn revealed the existence of the Borobudur. Work was thus begun on the task of cleaning the monument of all the eroding vegetation. But it was not until 1907 that a major restoration programme was commenced, with the prime objective of curbing the destructive force of rainwater.*

69 left and top right *In May, during full moon, the* waicak *festival commemorating the birth of Buddha is held in the temple of Borobudur. It involves processions, prayers and chanting by pilgrims and monks wearing saffron yellow robes. A particularly moving moment comes at dusk when pilgrims in procession make their way along corridors and terraces to the very top of the temple. It is said that the name Borobudur originates from the term* Bhumisanbharabhudara *with which it was once identified, meaning the "Mountain of Virtues of the Ten Stages of the Bodhisattva". Some authorities believe instead that the name derives from two words:* bara *and* budur. Bara - *from the Sanskrit* vihara - *means "group of temples, monasteries and dormitories".* Budur - *from the Balinese word* beduhur -, *means "over".*

70 top left *Van Erp, a Dutch engineer, led the restoration work and he succeeded in restoring the top three terraces to their former splendour. However, this left unsolved the problems concerned with the stability of the entire complex and the conservation of its reliefs. The temple had been built on a hill top, which was entirely covered by its various structures; it gradually started sinking onto its foundations and risked caving in.*

70 centre left *In 1955 the Indonesian government appealed to UNESCO for financial aid and technical specialists to help save Borobudur. In 1965 these two institutions launched a joint appeal to international experts, to develop a plan for the temple's complete restoration. The project (costing a total of 50 billion*

70 centre *With its quadrangular pyramid structure (138 feet high and sides 403 feet in length) enclosing the top of a small hill, the Borobudur has the form of the stupa, the temple mountain. The entire monument is comprised of seven tiers, of which two are part of the supporting quadrangular base platform. Rising from this platform, in steps, are four symmetrical galleries. In the centre of the four sides is a staircase (one for each cardinal point) giving access to the upper galleries. Carved over the entranceways and niches is the* kalamakara *demon motif.*

70 right *The walls of the four enclosed galleries of the Borobudur are decorated with no fewer than 1,460 panels of reliefs relating events in the life of the Buddha. In niches in the panels there are 504*

rupees) finally got underway in 1975: it involved dismantling the walls and balustrades of the first four terraces, treating the pieces of stone one by one to stop the corrosive action of the lichens, stabilizing the base with new concrete foundations and incorporating a complex and effective rainwater drainage system.

70 bottom left *A computer database was set up containing 300,000 items of information regarding the 3 million pieces of stone that together form the entire monument of Borobudur. The carved panels relating tales of the Buddha and all the other parts of the temple were then dismantled one by one, to be returned to their original place only upon completion of the work, in 1982-83.*

seated Buddha images. Opening out above the top gallery is a platform which forms the base of three circular terraces, with 72 perforated stupas.

71 *The stupas of the Borobudur complex are bell-shaped relic structures resting on a pedestal; a pole is fixed in the centre of their flat upper surface. They contain statues of meditative Buddhas: there are 32 on the first terrace, 24 on the second and 16 on the third. On the very summit of the temple, at the centre of the uppermost terrace, is a huge enclosed stupa. The Borobudur has a profound symbolic meaning, connected with the religious ideals of Mahayana Buddhism. It is conceived as a* mandala *(graphic mystic symbol of the universe) in which the square (base and galleries) represents the Earth and the circle (circular terraces) the Heavens.*

72-73 *Prambanan is the name given to the large group of Hindu temples and burial chambers of kings of antiquity situated a short distance from Yogyakarta, in a region endowed with many archaeological sites. These monuments testify to the religious, social and cultural pre-eminence of this area from the 8th to the 10th century A.D. An initial attempt to clean and restore the temples was made in 1855. But it was not until 1937 that extensive restoration work began, bringing to light the temples dedicated to Brahma, Vishnu and Siva and, later, part of the 240 candis originally built at this site. Candi Loro Jonggrang - as Prambanan is also commonly known - was named after the legendary princess whose hand in marriage was asked for by the giant Bantung Bondowoso, known for his supernatural powers.*

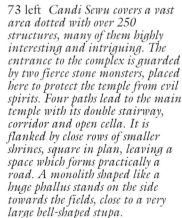

73 left *Candi Sewu covers a vast area dotted with over 250 structures, many of them highly interesting and intriguing. The entrance to the complex is guarded by two fierce stone monsters, placed here to protect the temple from evil spirits. Four paths lead to the main temple with its double stairway, corridor and open cella. It is flanked by close rows of smaller shrines, square in plan, leaving a space which forms practically a road. A monolith shaped like a huge phallus stands on the side towards the fields, close to a very large bell-shaped stupa.*

73 right *Candi Loro Jonggrang is dedicated to the Trimurti, which represents the highest deities of the Hindu religion: Siva (the god of eternity), Brahma (the god of creation) and Vishnu (the god who indicates the way to perfection). The temple was also the solemn burial place of kings and other court dignitaries: beneath each statue of a god is a hole in which a stone jar rests on a pile of charcoal, animal bones and earth. The ashes of the dead were placed inside this jar, together with jewels, coins, gold leaf and more earth and charcoal. The statues of the deities were carved in the likeness of the kings and members of their family, to ensure a constant link between the dead and the living.*

74-75 *The Prambanan complex is a material re-creation of the world of the gods, while the various temples together symbolize the cosmos: the lower parts of the structure were used to celebrate religious rites, the upper parts were reserved for the deities. The temple complex was originally comprised of 8 candis, arranged in hierarchical order, and 224 burial shrines (now in ruins), surrounded by three square terraces, the largest of which had sides about 1,312 feet long.*

75 centre *The five candis grouped together in the central part of the Dieng Plateau are named after heroes of the Mahabharatha (Semar, Arjuna, Srikandi, Puntadewa and Sembadra). They are small buildings containing a square cell resting on a plinth and preceded by a vestibule; they are almost completely roofless. The candis are decorated with relief carvings in which the kalamakara motif is a prominent feature (kala is the stylized lion,* makara *an imaginary animal of Hindu mythology): placed over door frames, it served to protect against evil spirits; it also symbolized the rainbow, the ideal bridge between the earthly and celestial worlds. Frequently found too are images of vehicles used by the deities. These sculptures are known to be of ancient origin: the temples, dedicated to the cult of Siva, are among the very oldest on Java.*

75 top right *Candi Sukuh is located 22 miles from the town of Solo. Its huge pyramid-shaped structure, resting on three platforms, clads the slopes of Mt. Lawu. With its terraces, steep steps and the use of stone, it bears a close resemblance to Central American Maya pyramids. Built between 1416 and 1459, the temple was dedicated to the legendary hero Bima, from the epic poem Mahabharatha, as well as to the cult of the dead and fertility: its relief carvings contain numerous phallic and erotic symbols.*

75 bottom right *The "Water Castle" in Yogyakarta - situated a short way from the Kraton - was built in the 18th century as a pleasure garden for the sultan and his dignitaries. With its white walls, towers, pavilions, ponds and bathing pools, it is in some way reminiscent of Moorish Spain.*

76 top *Tomok is situated on Samosir island in Lake Toba, Sumatra. In the higher part of the village are tombs of ancient kings of Samosir, who still figure large in the local cult. Many of these stone coffins are indeed monumental, some richly carved with human figures, others shaped like the prow of a boat or a Batak house. Casting welcome shade over the tombs are giant trees with gnarled roots protruding from the ground. A short way on, to the left, is a sacred enclosure with small stone figures depicting a ritual ceremony: above are the king and queen, at the sides musicians and a procession of worshippers. Two of them are portrayed in the act of self-sacrifice (testifying to the ancient Batak practice of human sacrifice).*

76 bottom *West Sumba, in the Lesser Sunda islands, is known for its megalithic tombs. Beside them stand totemic statues, densely carved with images of the many deities of the local animist religion. The focal point of this religion is the* marapu: *gods, supernatural forces and spirits which form the celestial world. Also part of this world is the mythical ancestor who was the first member of each* kabizu *(a tribal clan). Offerings of flowers, food and betel are placed before the* kateda *(or altar) to exorcise evil spirits and invoke the protection of the gods.*

77 *At Narmada, on Lombok, is the splendid Summer Palace of the rajahs of Bali, built in 1727 by Anak Agung Gde Ngurah Karangasem; at the centre of its garden is Air Awet Muda, a holy spring reputed to bestow eternal youth.*

78-79 *Pura Besakih is the most important temple on Bali. Situated in the village of the same name, it comprises hundreds of dark pagoda-like towers (merus) with access through a single imposing entrance gate. Besakih is in fact a group of temples, one for each of the Balinese principalities. The rajahs of Buleleng, Bangli, Denpasar, Negara, Gianyar, Tabanan, Karangasem and Klungkung all contributed to the construction of the temples. Once a year (coinciding with full moon in the first quarter of the Balinese calendar) they come here in pilgrimage, bringing offerings on behalf of the entire population of Bali.*

79 top *The village of Batur, not far from Kintamani, is on the slopes of the volcano of the same name (Lake Batur is in the caldera itself). A disastrous eruption in 1917, followed by another in 1926, led to its practically total destruction. Since then Pura Batur - the main temple, with its towering, many-tiered* merus *- has undergone continuous reconstruction.*

79 centre *The temple of Tanah Lot is located 19 miles from Denpasar. It was built by Sang Hyang Nirartha, one of the last Hindu priests to come to Bali from Java, particularly remembered for his success in "re-converting" the islanders to orthodox beliefs and practices. The temple stands on a rocky outcrop just off the coast, completely surrounded by water at high tide. It can be reached on foot at low tide over a narrow strip of sand.*

79 bottom *The temple of Kubutambahan is situated along the road to Singaraja, the main town on Bali's north coast. It features some unusual reliefs, for example of cyclists, depicted in a style that reflects Balinese aesthetic taste, with abundant ornamentation, bunches of flowers and turban-wearing figures.*

80-81 *Uluwatu - in the far south of the Bukit Peninsula, in Bali - is a both unusual and spectacular sight. Dedicated to the spirits of the sea, this temple stands perched on a high cliff, on the very tip of a headland. Its buildings overlook the deep blue waters of the ocean and are immersed in lush equatorial vegetation, populated by holy - and sometimes aggressive - monkeys. Uluwatu may look like a rather wild spot but it is in fact easily accessible. This is one of the reasons why many devout Balinese pilgrims visit the temple, as well as the cosmopolitan tourists now very much present in this part of the island.*

The thousand faces of Indonesia

82 top *For no fewer than 21 primary goods, Indonesia is among the world's top 20 producers (in absolute figures); for fishing it occupies twelfth place. This rating speaks for itself about the importance of fish, both for the Indonesian economy and in the nation's diet. Many different types of fishing vessels are used, like the high-prowed, brightly coloured boats of fishermen from Probolinggo, in north-east Java.*

82 bottom *Water buffalo are the faithful companions of Indonesian peasant farmers. These patient, good-natured creatures with crescent-shaped horns and grey coats have the considerable strength needed to plough rice paddies, which are found in every corner of the archipelago and particularly on Bali, in the Tabanan region.*

83 *The young girls of Bali exude a radiant loveliness. On reaching puberty, they are the protagonists of two ceremonial occasions: tooth-filing and ritual purification. In the first case, their top incisors are filed. This is done to eliminate all risk of resemblance to evil spirits or animals (with sharp teeth) and to protect from the six most serious shortcomings of human nature: love of luxury and grandeur, sensual pleasure, indifference, laziness, indecision and attachment to worldly goods. The second ceremony is celebrated when a girl menstruates for the first time. She is considered impure and kept in isolation until the end of the period. Then she is dressed in finery for the solemn purification ceremony, performed by a priest and followed by festivities with singing, dancing, music and eating.*

84 top *Most prominent among the many types of* wayang *is* wayang kulit *(from the words* wayang, *"shadow", and* kulit, *"leather"). The protagonists of these plays are puppets made of hide, manipulated with bamboo or horn rods by the* dalang *(puppet master): an overhanging lamp projects the shadows onto the screen (a white cloth stretched across a vertical frame, called* kelir).

84 bottom *The two most common kinds of theatre are* ludruk *and* ketoprak. *The themes of the first are taken from mythology, history and everyday life; men and women swap roles to heighten the comic effect. The second is a form of melodrama originated in Yogyakarta which draws its repertoire from Javanese, Chinese and Arabian folklore; the actors are dressed in sumptuous costumes and masks, similar to those worn by* kraton *dancers.*

84-85 *Having evolved in past centuries with a ritual and religious role, dance appears to be an innate part of the Javanese spirit. It was seen in its grandest forms in dance-dramas performed in the* kratons *of central Java, accompanied by the music of the royal* pelong-gamelan. *Although originating from Hindu religious and cultural tenets, it differs greatly from the Indian dance idiom. Several famous schools of classical Javanese dance are still based in the* kratons, *the most important in Solo and Yogyakarta (although the styles taught in each vary enormously). The dances are accompanied by* gamelan *music, often integrated with voices reciting the stories enacted by the dancers who are dressed in elegant costumes, with heavily made-up faces.*

The bulls
of Madura

86 top *Practically opposite Surabaya is the large island of Madura: vaguely rectangular in shape, it is 99 miles long and 19 miles wide. The island's main claim to fame is its bulls and oxen: the locally bred bulls are splendid animals, the very finest specimens seen during the equally famous races* (kerapan sapi) *staged every year between August and October. The events bring the whole island to life and attract large numbers of visitors.*

86 bottom *Decked out with bells and colourful ribbons, the bulls are paraded through the streets of the main towns before being taken to the racing stadiums. Hordes of islanders and Javanese come to watch the races, enthusiastically cheering on their favourite (on which they have often placed large bets, sometimes legally, sometimes not).*

86-87 *The "jockeys" are 15 year-old boys who balance precariously on a rudimentary, wheeless wooden "chariot", which rests on the ground. The two bulls are held by their tails which the boys pull and manipulate like reins as they try to spur them forwards in this crazy, breakneck charge. Often the jockey ends up rolling in the dust while the harnessed pair continues the race amid the screams and shouts of the spectators. In spite of their weight (772-882 pounds), the bulls reach a speed of 28 miles per hour; the best time on record is 9 seconds over a 328-foot long course.*

Fish and rice, food of the Orient

88-89 *Stretching across gentle slopes in the Central Highlands of Java, between Bogor and Bandung, are vast plantations where finest-quality tea is grown and used to produce blends exported throughout the world. These plantations, and others growing coffee and tobacco, were established here by Dutch settlers in the early 19th century. The plantation industry changed the island's entire agricultural economy by introducing products for export, rather than for home consumption.*

89 *Young and old, men and women alike, everyone does their share of the day's work in the omnipresent ricefields of Bali which are both a feat of hydraulic engineering and a spectacle of natural geometry.*

90 *The seafaring populations who live along the southern coasts of Sulawesi may lack the hi-tech facilities of Western fishing fleets but they nonetheless make a major contribution to the huge catches of the Indonesian fishing industry.*

Fish is an important ingredient of the Indonesian diet. It is cooked in many ways, but especially fried (ikan goreng). Krupuk is made from shrimp mixed with wheat, rice and fish flour, shaped into a kind of thin, unleavened pizza.

91 *Fish are caught in many different ways: one commonly used system is to build floating bamboo islands from which an acetylene lamp is hung at night to attract squid and cuttle-fish. In the south* of Sulawesi are small boatyards which specialize in building prahu and pinisi, *traditional Indonesian vessels on which the hull planking is bound together without the use of metal nails.*

In the name of Allah

92-93 *It was thanks to merchants from Persia and Gujarat that the Muslim religion first took root in Indonesia, back in the 12th century. Its initial stronghold was on the west coast of Sumatra, where a small trading colony had been founded. From the 13th century onwards flourishing trade brought ever-larger Arab communities to the most important ports of Java, Borneo and Sumatra itself. As their trading activities took them further and further afield, so their religious influence spread and much of the Indonesian archipelago and Malay peninsula came to embrace the Muslim faith. Around the year 1450, the Indo-Javanese kingdoms were overthrown by the Arabs and Islamic sultanates were established in their place. Islam thus became the national religion.*

A link with the past

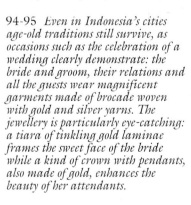

94-95 *Even in Indonesia's cities age-old traditions still survive, as occasions such as the celebration of a wedding clearly demonstrate: the bride and groom, their relations and all the guests wear magnificent garments made of brocade woven with gold and silver yarns. The jewellery is particularly eye-catching: a tiara of tinkling gold laminae frames the sweet face of the bride while a kind of crown with pendants, also made of gold, enhances the beauty of her attendants.*

Lords of Borneo

96-97 *Not only Tanjung Issui but much of Indonesian and Malaysian Borneo is inhabited by large numbers of Dayaks. There are many different Dayak groups, with communities differentiated by their lifestyles as well as the language they speak.*

97 top *Dayak tribes live in communal dwellings. Their very large longhouses (sometimes as much as 984 feet in length) are raised off the ground on stilts. They are built in the heart of the forest or close to rivers, as is the case of the village of Mancong which offers a typical example of a Dayak settlement.*

97 centre *The Mahakam River is one of the most important in Kalimantan (as the Indonesian part of Borneo is called). Along its course are stretches of rapids where the water turns to foaming white as it breaks against basalt boulders. Thanks to their skill in manoeuvring their long dugout canoes, the river is navigable by the local people.*

97 bottom *The Kenyah are a Dayak group who practise the elaborate art of tatooing. The men, in particular, have their bodies decorated with designs of animals and flowers and with geometric spiral patterns. Kenyah tribes continue to respect a hierarchical structure, with aristocrats and warriors at the top of the social pyramid.*

98 top *The rice harvest and other annual events which feature large in the day-to-day life of the Dayaks are occasions for colourful and lively festivities. The celebrations organized in the longhouses of Tanjung Issui are a particularly noteworthy example. A number of exceptionally distinctive dwellings have been restored by the Indonesian government and transformed into a kind of museum which relates the history of this proud and spirited people.*

98 bottom *For important festivities, nobles, village headmen and warriors wear their traditional dress. In the past festivities of this kind were organized to celebrate victory over enemy tribes. It was then common practice to cut off the heads of conquered enemies, which is why, even today, "bunches" of skulls, blackened by smoke, can be seen in longhouses, hanging from the beams above the communal veranda.*

99 *All women used to have designs of birds and spirits tatooed on their forearms. Now this is seen only amongst the older women, the younger ones having abandoned the practice. Ear-piercing is still common, with heavy earrings used to lengthen the lobes.*

The Torajas, offspring of the sea

100-101 *Local tradition has it that the Toraja descend from mariners from Pongko, who reached the shores of Sulawesi two or three thousand years ago in eight* lembang *(boats). This is the reason why their traditional house - the* tongkonan - *is shaped to resemble a boat, with bow and stern soaring skywards. Funeral rituals are attributed great importance by the Torajans and are believed to afford the deceased protection for an unlimited period of time.*

102 and 102-103 *Torajan tombs are cut in the faces of rocky cliffs. The elaborate but festive funeral ceremony takes place only after a vigil has been kept over the deceased for several months. The corpse is then wrapped in a shroud of red cloth embroidered with gold thread and placed in a coffin shaped like a boat, which is carried to the foot of the cliff. Skilled craftsmen carve a life-sized wooden effigy of the deceased - called* tau tau *- and dress it with clothes and ornaments similar to those worn by the person when alive. Like huge wooden puppets, the* tau tau *accompany the deceased in procession to their last resting place. The image, with eyes wide-open in a fixed stare, is then left on the sheer cliff face to guard the tomb and protect the soul on its journey into* pujo, *the kingdom of the dead.*

Rites and ceremonies

104-105 *The Balinese consider no action perfect unless it is accompanied by an offering to the gods, no day complete without the prescribed daily ritual; no week passes by without participation in a festival or some other social function. And so it continues, year in, year out. Life on Bali is thus interspersed with a succession of elaborate religious ceremonies: local dignitaries walk in procession, shielded from the sun by large parasols, women balance on their heads silver and gold trays with prestigious votive offerings, priests officiate at ceremonial rites. Only brahmins, who spend much of their existence studying theology, are able to acquire in-depth religious knowledge. Ordinary people are instead expected to simply believe, taking part in religious rites and following the precepts of their faith.*

106-107 *Funerals are festive occasions for the Balinese since they believe the death of the body marks the start of a new life for the soul. Cremation, considered a sacred duty, releases the soul which can then reach higher spheres and be reincarnated as another living creature. On the established day and following an elaborate ritual, corpses are taken from their temporary burial place and transferred to the cremation site. Here a large bamboo tower (often 66 feet high) representing the Balinese cosmos, is erected and adorned with floral garlands, colourful drapes and altars of the* sun. *Its large base, frequently built in the shape of a turtle, symbolizes the base which supports the world; on top of it is the* bale-balean *(the space between heaven and earth), comprised of a platform on which the sarcophagus containing the body is placed; last of all comes a roof formed of a series of graduated, pagoda-like tiers. The cremation tower for* sudra - *called* wadah - *has only one tier; for other castes it can have from three to eleven tiers, and is known as a* bade. *The sarcophagus is a carved wooden bull (for men) or cow (for women), which the corpse is put into before being set alight.*

108-109 *The splendid festival of* Melasti *takes place in Sanur, just one of the countless festivals held on the island of the gods. The people of Bali have two different systems for establishing the most propitious time for their rites: the* Caka *Hindu calendar (in which years are numbered) and the Balinese* Wuku *calendar (in which they are not numbered). The Caka is divided into 12 months; the phases of the new moon and full moon are indicated, as well as the most important religious festivities; each month is divided into 29 or 30 days but the years are not numbered in the same way as in the Western world. The Wuku is instead based on a more complex system: weeks can have from one to ten days, and the months vary in length too; the days are named after the planets of the solar system.*

The dances of good and evil

110 top *The forces of good and evil come face-to-face in the* baris *dance of which there are many variations, generally adaptations of* baris *rites. The dancers move keeping their knees apart, toes raised off the ground, spine straight, arms held above shoulder height, fluttering finger-tips bent backwards.*

110 bottom *Most Balinese dances have a religious meaning; they nearly always tell dramatic stories inspired by Hindu mythology and classic tales. Their appeal stems essentially from the attributes of the dancers: magnificent costumes, natural beauty, elaborate make-up and harmonious movements.*

110-111 *In the temple of the village of Pelintan, Ngurah Mandra - one of Bali's most renowned dance masters - goes through some steps of the extremely demanding* legong kraton *dance. Little girls begin the difficult learning process at the age of five and continue to practise and perform this elegant court dance until their early teens.*

111 top *The barong dance represents the struggle between good and evil. The barong - a mythical monster with a large body, four paws and a long, upward-pointing tail - symbolizes the forces of nature working to defend mankind, the glory of the sun and the benign spirits associated with white magic;* *he is engaged in a fierce battle against the witch* Rangda, *personifying the forces of evil, black magic and malevolent spirits. The story related has both magical and symbolic meanings; before each performance offerings are therefore made to the gods, to invoke their protection for the actors.*

112-113 *The* kecak *dance got its name from the sound repeated rhythmically and obsessively by a chorus of men crouched on the ground in concentric circles, without music. In their midst other men mime and dance episodes from the Ramayana by torchlight, while a narrator tells the story portrayed in the dance (which is also known as the monkey dance).*

111 centre *Mysterious, disquieting masks cover the faces of* topeng *dancers whose brightly coloured and ornate costumes attest to the creativity and imagination of the people of Bali.*

111 bottom Topeng *dancers wear masks and beautiful costumes but they must also be talented mime artists, able to make their bodies convey the many feelings of the characters they portray.* Topeng *comprises many old dances performed by a single actor, used to introduce a form of theatre which goes under the same name.*

Along the ocean's shores

114-115 *Along the coasts of Bali the shores are protected by what remains of the coral reef. Moored on the beaches are numerous* prahu *with bows that resemble a fish's snout, and colourful triangular sails: these seagoing dugout canoes with outriggers are the boats typically used by Balinese fishermen. They can also be rented to sail down to Seregan Island or the Bukit peninsula.*

116 *Labuhanbajo, on Flores, seems little more than a village but it is actually the capital town of this region, offering all the essential services. Many fishermen live here. The main street, Jalan Sudarso, runs parallel to the shore and everything - or almost - can be found here. Between the houses which skirt the beach, boatbuilders are at work.*

116-117 *"Sea gypsies" in* prahu *negotiate the waters around the island of Komodo. Originating mainly from the south of Sulawesi, they travel from island to island on these swift-moving vessels, often stopping on a particular shore and establishing a temporary home there, in a cluster of houses built on piles. When catches start to get meagre, they move on in search of richer fishing grounds.*

Manifestations of faith

118 left *On the profoundly Muslim island of Sumbawa the tenets of the Koran are devoutly respected, especially in the east where practically all women wear the* rimpu, *not unlike the* chador. *As long ago as the 11th century, Arab merchants came to these parts in search of spices and sandalwood. Small local principalities, tributaries of the Javanese Majapit dynasty, were converted to Islam in the 17th century by the Makassarese, who reduced them to subservience.*

118 right *The animist religion is deeply entrenched in the history and traditions of Sumba and many islanders still adhere to its beliefs today. Elaborate rituals are officiated by priest-doctors whose magic powers are thought to heal every kind of illness.*

119 *The intense but nervous glances of the women of Bima, on the island of Sumbawa, are a pointer to the way in which the fair sex is oppressed by the rigid rules of Islam.*

Rites of war in a land of peace

120 *Inhabitants of aboriginal origin first appeared on Timor some 14,000 years ago, followed by Australasians and peoples of Mongol origin. Today the Atoni and Tetum are the most numerous groups: the Atoni live in the mountainous regions and account for half the population of Timor Barat. The Tetum instead predominate in Timor Timur. Age-old traditions still survive here, for instance in the form of war dances that testify to the warlike nature of these peoples.*

121 left and bottom right *From all over the island of Sumba magnificent horsemen come to pit their strength in duels that have all the trappings of a medieval tournament. This equestrian battle - called* pasola *- is an annual fertility rite which recalls the most ancient traditions of the people of Sumba. Galloping on their horses, often hardly larger than ponies, the contestants fight with three spears which they thrust at their opponents as soon as the signal is given. The*

horses rear up and crash to the ground, often fatally wounded, with their riders. They believe that this bloody tribute is needed to placate the goddess Nyale and gain her protection.

121 top right *The war dance is a reminder of the times when belligerence was a predominating characteristic of the inhabitants of the island of Flores, and common to all the indigenous peoples of this part of Indonesia.*

122-123 *The Grand Baliem Valley covers an upland area of some 203 square miles in the interior of Irian Jaya. In the early morning it is swathed in a thick curtain of cloud which gives it a mysterious, ghostly appearance. The valley is drained by the Baliem River - from which it takes its name - whose muddy waters flow into the Arafura Sea. It is inhabited by the Dani, the best known tribe of the entire region. Farmers and warriors, they lived in total isolation until 1938 when the explorer Richard Archibold first landed his seaplane in the vicinity of Danau Habbema. Exploration of the region was interrupted by World War II and resumed only in 1954 when the first missionaries arrived here: from then onwards life in the valley began slowly to change. Within their traditional, fenced-in villages the Dani are self-sufficient. Besides huts used as the communal kitchen and for women's dwellings, each village has a men's house and an enclosure for pigs; the village population usually numbers about 20-30 people. The houses are circular with arched roofs. The men, who are almost always completely naked, wear the* horim *(penis sheath); they also cover their hair and body with pig fat and soot, as a means of protection against insect bites and the cold of night. Polygamy is the traditional matrimonial system practised by the Dani: a man has as many wives as he can accommodate in his house and can afford to buy.*

124-125 and 125 The town of Agats is situated in the south-east of Irian Jaya, on the Arafura Sea, at a point where the Baliem River forms marshes, lagoons and a muddy estuary. The area around Agats is the homeland of the Asmat, formerly headhunters and cannibals, now predominantly converts to Christianity. The government in Jakarta has forced them to abandon their nomadic life, to wear clothes and to live in permanent settlements where there are schools, churches, mosques and hospitals. Many Asmat are now employed as poorly paid loggers by multinational timber companies. Large numbers of them have taken refuge in more inaccessible, impervious parts of the country where they continue to adopt the traditional lifestyle of their ancestors.

126-127 For the Asmat - still primarily hunter-gatherers who live on what they can find and catch in the forests of their homeland - bows and arrows are an essential weapon as well as a means of obtaining food. They also use long spears which they decorate with multi-coloured bird feathers. Some of the Asmat paint long white stripes on their bodies, as ornamentation.

128 Flores, "island of flowers", is a strip of land stretching 224 miles from Rinca in the west to Adonara in the east (but measuring only between 7 and 43 miles from north to south). Crossing it from Labuhanbajo to Larantuka is the Trans-Flores Highway (435 miles), a kind of roller-coaster from which travellers can enjoy views of amazingly beautiful landscapes strewn with verdant rice fields.

Illustration credits

Marcello Bertinetti / Archivio White Star: Back cover, pages 8, 24 bottom, 26-27, 35 top e bottom, 36 bottom, 36-37, 39 top, 44-45, 48-4950, 51, 60 bottom, 67, 68, 69, 70, 71, 78, 79, 83, 110, 111, 112-113, 115, 116-117, 118 left, 119.

Bruno Barbier / The Emispheres: page 42-43, 43 top

Michele Bella: pages 4-5, 12-13, 61, 75 bottom, 77, 104 bottom.

Alain Benainous / Agenzia Gamma: page 65.

Peter Charlesworth / The Stock House: page 19 bottom.

Alain Compost / Bruce Coleman: page 25

E. Coppola / Panda Photo: page 54 bottom, 116.

Gerald Cubitt - Bruce Coleman: pages 54-55, 102-103.

G. Cubiti / Panda Photo: page 122-123.

Paolo Curto / The Image Bank: pages 6-7.

Georgette Douwma / Planet Earth: page 24 top.

Jean Leo Dugast / The Stock House: page 101 top.

Foschi / Focus Team: pages 30 top, 54 al centro, 105 bottom.

Alexander Frank - BildarchivSteffens: pages 76 top, 105 top left.

Bertrand Gardel / Emispheres: pages 31, 46, 88-89, 105 top right.

Marais - Gaussen / Agenzia Franca Speranza: pages 86, 87.

Laurent Giraudou / Anzenberg / Ag. Franca Speranza: Front cover.

Photo Bank: pages 1, 2-3, 16-17, 18, 19 top, 22-23, 28-29, 32-33, 34-35, 38 bottom, 39 bottom, 40-41, 43 bottom, 47, 52-53, 54 top, 56, 57, 58-59, 62 bottom, 64 bottom, 72, 73, 75 top, 76 bottom, 82 bottom, 84-85, 90, 91, 92-93, 94, 95, 96, 97, 98, 101 al centro e bottom, 108-109, 114-115, 118 right, 120, 121, 122, 124-125, 126-127.

David M. Hayes / The Stock House: page 62 al centro.

J. C. Munoz / Panda Photo: page 35 centre.

Chuck O'rear / The Stock House: pages 84 bottom, 99, 102, 125.

Andrea Pistolesi: pages 14-15, 60 top, 62 top, 64 top, 80-81, 82 top, 104 top, 106, 107, 111 top.

Lincoln Poiter / The Stock House: page 84 top.

Joei Racocha / BildarchiveSteffens: pages 74-75.

Guido Alberto Rossi / The Image Bank: pages 9, 33 top e bottom, 62-63, 66, 100-101.

G. Saltini - G. Castaldi / Panda Photo: page 36 top.

Cyril I. Schwart - The Image Bank: page 89.

Ken Straiton / The Stock House: page 30 bottom.

Pietro Tarallo: page 128

Steve Vidler / The Stock House: page 21.

Konrad Wothe / The Image Bank: page 38 top.